TRAILER TRASH

SELECTED BY
ROBIN COSTE LEWIS
FOR THE 2016 KORE PRESS
FIRST BOOK AWARD
IN POETRY

PRAISE FOR TRAILER TRASH

Robin Coste Lewis

When I read the title of this collection, I'll admit it: I didn't want to read it. I thought—obnoxiously—that I knew what I would find before turning its first page: cute, pink poems about poverty—which is to say, a style of writing I wanted to avoid completely. I was wholly unprepared for the exceptional skill and aesthetic courage I encountered when I opened the book, skill and courage that remained from the first line to the last. It is so much easier to perform rather than to be honest. You can offer the world a mask, then walk away, pretending to be somewhere, someone. This is especially true when one is poor, or a woman. But from beginning to end, these poems about both are neither cute, nor nice. They are strong, quiet, new, unapologetic, even ruthless in their refusal to play any role, including "girl" or "poor." Which is to say, July Westhale constantly creates wholly unfamiliar constructions that run back and forth between that pole of both exquisite and horrifying with courageous agility. Evoking the language of myth, history, sociology, Westhale takes a sign as overused as "trailer trash" and utterly destroys that myth (or is it nightmare?) completely. Furthermore, she refuses to look away from the true complexity of gender and poverty, or more specifically, what it actually means to grow up both poor and girl. It isn't new—class analysis—of course not. Indeed, one could argue that class is precisely what women within patriarchy write. What else could we write, century after century, when it took us so long to own property or even vote? That's called a tradition. But what's exciting for me is I know this collection, "Trailer Trash," will take its rightful place within this exquisite history. What's even more thrilling, however, is the awareness that this voice is completely distinct, these narratives, this terrain belong only to the narrators who tell them. And that's something that one can never force, nor fake. Indeed, perhaps the greatest gifts of this collection are that it does not run from the complexities of class and gender, nor the Athenian feat of locating unpretentious, deeply psychological lyric to render them.

TRAILER

TRASH

JULY WESTHALE

KORE PRESS   TUCSON   2018

Celebrating 25 Years!
Standing by women's words since 1993
Kore Press, Inc., Tucson, Arizona USA
www.korepress.org

Cover photograph, "Untitled" (2014), by Julia Sparenberg
Design by James Meetze

We express gratitude to the Arts Foundation for Tucson and Southern
Arizona, the Arizona Commission on the Arts, and to individuals for
support to make this Kore Press publication possible.

ISBN 978-1-888553-94-9

Library of Congress Cataloging-in-Publication Data:

Names: Westhale, July, author.
Title: Trailer trash / By July Westhale.
Description: Tucson, AZ : Kore Press, 2017.
Identifiers: LCCN 2017055691 | ISBN 9781888553949 (softcover)
Classification: LCC PS3623.E8493 A6 2017 | DDC 811/.6--dc23
LC record available at https://lccn.loc.gov/2017055691

For Mr. Mac
(Sept. 6, 1943 - Feb. 21, 2009)

&

Rebecca Gerdes
(Dec. 18, 1958 - Jan. 25, 1992)

TABLE OF CONTENTS

Part III

Notes

I.

Blythe, California

"Where you come from is gone, where you thought you were going to never was there, and where you are is no good unless you can get away from it."

—FLANNERY O'CONNOR

ARS POETICA

One would like to see oneself walking through the forest as two girls,
      along a creek, the golden carp under the ice like blurred poppies.
The tall, hooded girl will extend a basket, offering bread and water, a kindly
      face and a thick cloak.
The other is small, with sly hands. She will eat her fill, wrap herself
      in the warmth of the wool cloak, cut a branch from a tree.
Whittling the end to a point, she will pull the arrow back, and shoot it
      into the throat of the hooded girl. She will retrieve the basket.

INTOLERABLE OBJECTS / TOMATO

The first was sliced thick, watery and viscous
with seedy mire, menses on Irish thighs.

Imagine an immaculate kitchen window:
a picture show with a poodle skirt of cumulus.

Lettuce, now an irreparable mess, lies
complicit on a plate, smelling of clammy nightshades.

Once I was a hothouse gone to seed
in a trailer park in Blythe, the sky

vermillion in airlessness, in suffocating
sunsets of dust and pesticides,

our food dead and gone. The dinner table
was the color of a beetle trapped in sap.

If I sit long enough, merciful troops
of aphids arrive, steady in the night, and I am allowed

to heave the scarlet filth from dishware
to toilet drain, pooling blood in the basin.

In the yard, a woman paid to care
feeds our soiled underwear to potbelly pigs.

CROP DUSTERS

When I woke up, I couldn't tell which of my sisters I'd become.
We smelled of eggs, and I broke us by leaving the trailer.
If you can, pretend the alfalfa field is the Celestial City.
A man, surely a prophet, walks his dog in a pilling robe.
He is the color of sky. His dog carries the truth in its leg.
The truth is a hard knot, difficult to rub out.
The planes, by now, have come and left us a magic trail.
The trail is a beanstalk to the Lord, and we must have faith.
Our water browns after the Lord's planes come, but we are faithful.
If I had to guess, I'd say John the Baptist. He'd have baptized
a sick dog. He'd have believed a sick dog could find the beanstalk.
Every morning, the air is as thick as syrup from a pitcher.
It is quiet, sliced up, and ready to digest, like a hymn.
The hymnal of the morning moves North, to Eagle Mountain.
Our melon fields have been blessed by the Lord.
We and our canals are filth waiting to be turned to loaves.

SAGUAROS

Blythe rises in welts.

It pinches California and my mother,
the menstruating horizon between the two.

Thus it was with her. She, a cloud: long
and placed perfectly. Sky strong and full
of torn cornflower blue.
Before me, the babies were born
as still and silent as mercury. A victory
for her, when her field caught seed
and bloomed startlingly open—

I was born in a dry world, and we lived
as chasms among men, saguaros
with hundreds of years holding rain;
the same, in a sense as wild beasts
in battle, who want for water.

We were mistaken in taking
from the cracked ground, brown
and spent. Forget men.
We were better off withholding.

I tell you this because she's gone, now,
and you are a kind and forgiving reader,
seeking truth.

For truth, I say I remember
this mother, the mother of my nights
bringing home a jackrabbit,
pulling a tooth trap from its pelage to slit
the pregnant belly, knowing
the body to be a stasis and the desert a hell,
and the knife the only bridge between the two.

HEAVEN, THAT DAY-OLD BREAD

Stars are melting in heavy pours of salt
or sweet cream, a magnificent lipid
looking like curdled clouds.
The city is concerned. Were it cloudless,
there'd be a watchman's visibility
                            and a cricket's footfall. What a terrible joke.
Acid ground kisses women's feet
as they coo away. On TV, the world consumes.

The city releases a sonorous belch
and the grounds smells of gaseous almonds.
A fool, a poet, comparing a moon to a clitoris,
misses the night bus's *tsk*
                    and the disappointment is fragrant. A raccoon pawing
grocery garbage is the only news, a lumbering
ombrologist in the pathological gloaming.

I was raised with the chewed-out scents of California,
                            and a rhinestone horizon.
What if the sky is no different in a city than from a field?
That it is my constitution that has seen spots of lily-livered
mold, calling a moon vestigial and a pleasure?
                            I embarrass myself.
When a star melts, it ruins the lot, like pissing
on the last finished geranium in a watercolor.

Somewhere, surely a piano is banged upon.
A player looks, startled in her recognition
                    of something familiar, but annihilating.

DEAD MOM

She opened her mouth.

In this story, the child makes a house out of a box,
a river from a pile of dead leaves,
a companion from a cloud formation,
and a self of shifting ponds.
Her parents are lost in the fog
on a train somewhere in the mountains,
and when she sleeps, she does so well.

There is a word for adopted children,
they are called *fawns*. The woods are full of them,
and their biggest adversary is the night,
and the owls who call to mice as they shrink away,
and large sequoias who burn themselves as sacrifice.

In a story she dreams at home in a bed,
a child made a home in a soft trunk
in a clearing of sword ferns. It is full
of fat worms and sleeping possums,
and the stars are stored away somewhere,
spinning and sparking against each other.
And when they die, she knows nothing of it.

CHOPIN'S FUNERAL MARCH

Grandmother's mouth vowels the air. The mother
is not underwater, but under soil. No one surfaces
from under stones but the mother's daughter, an heir
to the living poke-grass and fresh dirt.

Not underwater but under soil. No one surfaces
except through hymns, and the day takes back
the living poke-grass and fresh dirt.
Sleep croons a peaty and unpleasant note

and except through hymns, when the day takes back
the phone, as it did what it was asked, dialing 9-1-1-1-1-1—
sleep croons a peaty and unpleasant note,
like a moth the granddaughter swallowed, knowing nothing.

A mother has no point of view. She's dead.
The grandmother's mouth vowels air, above a mother
cold in January rain, cold in her bed
under stones and the mother's daughter, an heir.

WAKE

Some night, dad and I
drive all evening through the mirage—

                          wet, but not exactly.

To the eyes, a great oasis
in a great desert. The eyes fail. The road fails.
Joking, in this moment, fails, and we
keep the radio between us.

The Colorado River is getting big
in the britches, stepping on Blythe
like that. All wild goose and border.

                         Some country, hey kiddo?

The lie uplifts us. Our cotton
hasn't been watered all year, and our towns
are blossoms of mosquitos.

In death, heaven forgives us. Heaven
must be somewhere past the Sun.
Heaven must have farmers. Someone
must know how to irrigate.

When we are both adults, I take
the wheel. The light is buoyant
in eventide. The whole world
is ink.

Flash, and then flood. Then a car,

                  then a raft.

COOTIE CATCHER

I. Green

Pick a number. Any number.

We'd set about to build a paper boat,
but our futures are more fascinating.
We pretend the duo paper is us, sister,
born six weeks apart—adopted twins,
winning the strangest gestation story ever told.

Besides, a cootie catcher could float.
A cootie catcher could be salvation to a locust,
or a June bug in distress at sea, our sea.
The sea is a muddied puddle, stretched shallow as a sandfish.

We fold our friends: the cootie catchers, the frogs,
the tulips, the schooners.
                              Who taught you origami, anyway?

II. Yellow

To make a catcher, you must have a square.
You must have the same length of sides. You must
cut your rectangle into a shape like a window,
so it opens perfect. You could risk
everything. You could unfold a flap
and predict niceness. What do children know
of niceness?

These are not the future. These are not religion. These are entertainment.

III. Red

Our town is leave-able.
Our uncle left that summer,
floating in an irrigation canal we all
fished in, a big bloat.
He'd been drunk, and dreaming
of carp. We ate the carp, carp is poor
folks' food. We take communion
regularly. This is no different.

LOVE ARRIVED MAY FIND US SOMEPLACE ELSE

for Caleb

The news did not shock the town,
used to being shocked, as one who wants
is used to being turned away.

Still, it was a good deal
to take in, though I was not the one
pregnant, and my sister
was sure in her resolve to keep it.

That summer, I was determined to fall from very tall bridge or sink under
      a heavy lake, string pills with thread for a necklace, and eat them
while dancing. I was no longer able to deal with having been raped. During
      which my sister grew thick, with a strange tadpole swimming in our
shared river.

I wanted
and she wanted
and he wanted, though he knew nothing
of want, not yet born
and we knew nothing of boys,
much less men.

Let's change the story, rewrite the foreshadow, strengthen the characters,
      forego the ending. It is with exclamations he is sentenced to the
world. On the way from the hospital, I gave him the commas of my fingers,
      to slow him. Without pause, he pulled them to his mouth, resolved to
keep them.

I want, but I know nothing—
understand nothing. Love
arrived may find us someplace else:
either born, or sleeping,
and what choice have we
but to rise, and outstretch,
say we planned for this,
and how good of you, to come at last.

OBITUARY OF AN UNKNOWN WOMAN

Nora Horowitz has crossed today says Sunday
says the paper at the corner market
where I am walking my girlfriend's frantic
dog and suddenly I see her faceless obituary
Nora's not my girlfriend's
nor her dog's though I wouldn't put it past her
Nora I don't even know you
I must have almost known you
the relief is dreadful dear God I bet
we went to the same church where my granddaddy
still preaches Nora I mean it's truly awful
that you're dead Nora not my granddaddy
he can put a sermon together real nicely
I bet if I asked right now he'd pray for you
Nora I bet we would have fallen in love
I really mean it I reckon we'd have fallen
for each other in the library under Raymond Carver's
This is What We Talk About When We Talk About Love
Nora in my heart of hearts I know you look
exactly like Jennifer Beals in *Flashdance* you've got to
have the same inside grace that turns your smile lines
into burning branches and torches me Nora
you were brought into the world
in Eagle Mountain where the planes rest their heads
so maybe the cancer is something you inherited
Nora what I'm saying is maybe you didn't summer with it
at the Riverside County YMCA or drink it long
and insatiably during El Niño's baked asphalt years
when the ground steamed up and up but there was nothing
no water no trail of mirage along the roads
and everyone and their mother was driving without

air conditioning Nora because air conditioning
would have made the transmission kick the bucket
Nora I bet you would have liked our life together
no more clapboard and tin houses no more
hissing squawking planes over cockcrow no more
apocalyptical evangelism except maybe my granddaddy's
occasionally but only if we came back to this shithole town
Nora I bet you would have a real foul mouth
I bet your foul mouth could have met mine in the middle
and they could have battled Nora
I bet you would be serious about your coffee
and you would greet me in the morning
quiet and statue-like on account of the absence
of planes and you would say *I made you
this cuppa and it's shit-your-pants strong*
and take me hard and reverently
against the dinette and make my eyes go green
behind the lids, take me as a thrip
takes a seedling cotton curling my body
upwards to meet you where you have crossed
to the Elysian fields and wait with a smirk—

Tell me, what of faith? That weather inside,
that wrecks and sings of Calvary,
that is part wind, part chill, and part something
to be watched from a small room,
a window. The answer
is a great, rusted turn of the bow:
devotion to air, because there is nothing
to see, and everything to freeze.

TRAILER TRASH

You won't believe the life you'll be asked to live.
—Brian Teare

The thing about trash is trash is work. Trash is
a chore. Trash needs cleansing. Trash needs hiding,
shaping, repurposing. *What a dump*
the inspector says. Our homes are a tin crown
of sonnets, light upon them even in night,
cresting our corrugated roofs like a slant rhyme.

Is it not conquest, to own the refuse of others?
It is not somewhat reluctantly graceful, to be
thrown away? Are we not the pride of our community?

The other side sent planes. *For bugs*
the inspector says. It is 1989, and the cotton
is a crown of holey shirts, stained
at the armpits. We toe the right of red.
We are settlers of glory, and chosen. My sisters

appraise our stolen divinity like heiresses,
who have known their whole life of what waits for them.

Were we crow, or scarecrow? Do we frighten
or feast, as the other side kindly kills
our vermin?

We're scarecrow.

Wearing the clothes of those
who position us. We wave
regally, graciously, to our peons in planes.
They whir, soft as silk, the pilot faceless.

Does he know us as people, or sticks
as our burnished arms sway, moving
like stalks among birdlessness?

II.

Pharaohs and Men

"Don't go. Let me show you what it looks like when surrender, and an instinct not to, run side by side."

—CARL PHILIPS

CHAPEL

Not a word was a word. The book
     disagrees. I lived by this. Still
live by it. I did not have a throat
     boiled with song. Years ago,
I entered a storage shed, a chapel
     of untouchables. My mother
had left behind many words—journals,
     with twenty-two years of silt coating. Books,
not books I'd chose, not lullabies.
     She seemed to see my life before my eyes
opened, put down a road, and left me there.

THERE IS NO ROOM FOR JESUS IN THIS CITY

take me to the bricks of light,
they cried, *those walls of backlit crosses.*
—Wayne Miller

All day long the buildings sleep, and dream of the people in them.

When the sun shrugs its shoulders into the horizon,

the world is full and the evening that passes, promising.

I was lying just then. There is nothing hopeful

about being a bringer of light. What do I know of cities? Urbanity

makes a mess of skies, leaving stoplights scabbing overhead.

Before the drought, the airspace was a gash of clouds.

It rained so much the city believed itself clean. It will never

be clean. From inside the walls, people played Jericho.

This was before the dearth. This is why the fields are safer.

The city would never flood—that isn't the way, the truth,

or the light. Where I come from, promises are kept.

Every night, the city sleeps loudly, snoring sirens.

The vehement whirring of mechanical birds attempts to lull,

to shine nightlights so we might find our way. We will never

find our way. There is just sleep, nothing but sleep.

Child, would you ride along
swinging your arms, reciting lessons
for tests: shapes, colors, letters—
how things fit? Would you remember
what came after what, the place
of things, the view out the window
as your town burned by? Child
are you alone? Do others sit
beside you on the road home?
When you were left
to take the bus, what was it
you were left with?

Child, if you knew what time was,
if you knew what time could be,
the shape of it, the color, the spelling—
if you knew how things fit, if you
knew to repurpose memory to serve you,
then it might have saved you,
child. Just a child, a mild-mannered
passenger on a bright bus heading home.

Child, if you had all the time, all the time
as a beautiful parade, an extra lunch, too
much saved and scavenged time, if you borrowed
all the time from others, if you pretended
you could drive a car, and that time was hog-tied
in the trunk of it, if you could braid time
into your hair, or draw it so that you might
show it to other children and say
this is time, this is all the time

because you had it, then maybe you would
believe you came from an ancestry
of time, that everyone before you owned
time, that time has never been scarce
in your blood, that time has been a part
of your story since time itself. And maybe, then,
there would be reason enough to believe
you had taken everything, and you could believe it
when they tell you your mother has plumb run out.

Every Sunday, we think about driving to church,
but instead end up fucking
execution style: gruesomely, and against a wall.
I get caught in the headlights
of our love, and moon about intersections
like a lost traffic cone, orange and useless.
It's always the same ending: our streets
slick and blurry in the spectacular
light of accidents, like artic borealis.
I ask far too much of us, to be a destination where
I meant to leave a lamentation,
I meant to shake a psalm from your skin, but no—
In reality, we are earnest in our erasure, truthful
as a salt-eaten screen door, and as loud.

DEAD MOM, OR HOW NEWS TRAVELS IN A SMALL TOWN

You are so kind
to sit here, and watch
the fields disappear. She was
going to come pick me
up from school today,
but I've only just begun.
I have so many school days
left. Look, there is cotton,
like a soft place to sleep.
There is alfalfa. Thrip
eat seedlings. But not today.
I'll arrive safely at my bus stop,
and you yours.
It's good of you to sit
beside me, because my mother
will be glad I had the company.
I will be speedy now. I will
get off at the alfalfa,
meet sleep, and not disappoint
the cotton, since anyone could overdose—
How beautiful the bus ride is.
Can you see the trees there,
blurs of finger paint?
How kind you are, to sit
beside me. A woman died,
you say, of an overdose.
This is poor country. Addiction
is common. She might have been
anyone's mother. That letter,
in cursive, you show me—
that you should sit beside me, that

you should come home
quickly. I find it exceptionally sweet.
This would be news
—it couldn't be her. She wouldn't
leave when I have just started kindergarten.
Our names together like that—
they are just names. Many people have them.

DONNER PASS, 2012

> *May we with Gods help spend the comeing [sic] year better than*
> *the past which we purpose to do if Almighty God deliver us from*
> *our present dreadful situation.*
> —the diary of Patrick Breen, December 31, 1846

Knowing you were waiting
on the other side of it,

                my train
cut through the thickly-sliced fat
of snow

       to the bone. The wheels sang
my love is good my love is good.

                    And then, nothing.

—

and then, a boulder. And then
we were pinned

            to the tracks. We were honest:
we were the sort of folks
who'd believe a man when he said

                      shortcut
without ever having taken it himself.

—

hearts go bad

        like something open on a shelf
that's all. Your letter, a letter

              with boxes in it, being packed.

—

We couldn't move
        if we wanted to,
so we call disaster
        by its married name:
a setback, a small delay—

    —

I forgive you.
You, who have so much
to be forgiven for.
        The universe
is a graceless one. Who killed them
        but their own,
and where did they go
        with all of the choicest cuts?

THE FLOWER CARRIER

If I could not have made this garden beautiful
I wouldn't understand your suffering,
nor care for each the same, inflamed way.
—Paisley Rekdal

She has the tired grace
of a nun who has been up
all night, self-flagellating.

Standing beside the painting
without standing it.

It is Rivera's *Flower Carrier*. We know this.
Not everyone withstands the weight
of flowers. The man knows it. His first words
in the morning are *my flowers*.

Did they dry up in the night, turning
away from him in their beds?
Did they wither with touch?
Die from a stroke of heat, or a fallen frost?

They are a burden, and he keels under them
 as his wife cups the basket. He crawls away.

The nun—my girlfriend—is before the man.
I go to her, touching the world
of her breasts to feel the weave of stitching.
She cups them. Her breath is thick as pollen.

PINOCHET SPEAKS FROM HIS CASKET

December 10ʰ, 2006

There was a strike. That much was obvious.

Papers in the air, those bright burnt birds.

And somewhere, a young face— I know it not,
came into my dead, blurred vision, staying a spell,
waving a grenade, biting into it as if
it were a pomegranate. And when I chanced

to meet his eye, he strayed to the stars
on my breast, my decorated bronze
and golden leaves—and why
was I in such a small box, such a sheath
to hold a sword this size? I see only half
the world from here, the sky a processional
I never asked for: quiet, oppressive.

When my boy Osvaldo was young and fearful
of lightning that struck the field,
the terrible cracking of thunder, like a sheet
pulled crisp over a cold bed—I
brought him into my arms, said *We are not large enough
to be harmed*, while the wind toughened around us.
My boy, my boy, named for me, howled.
And looked, when I thought of it, like burnt wheat.

The young man with the grenade speaks, crying
a call and response that others join. A boy once.

He has died, he said.

I've died? I think.

My window quickly fills with heavy rain,
mucous and spit, and all my boys
clutch newsprint emblazed my face.
Not a leaf moves in this country without me knowing—

MARRIED MEN (DADDY ISSUES)

I want the pharaohs, but there's only men.
—Neko Case

The ring is inside a box
not meant for a ring.

The Cadillac is white.
The day has no wet in it.

Flowers are put out like one
arranging tiny lingerie.

It's Las Vegas in the mind,
so everything stays there.

It's honor. It's horror. Divorce,
fake as it is, bloody on the dash.

A wife is a wife is a wife
is a daughter. I make no vows

with the failure of our salvation.
At sea, mariners would say

this is a sure thing,
shipwreck, and be done with it.

HYMN

Have mercy, she who makes the morning
          gone: among fits, just splits. I am
broken in egret-colored sheets, in dust
          my waking makes. I did not leave her.
Ever slowly, I count. Keep the reel
          reeling as a second, long look. Compose
while she decomposes. Backward
          symphony. There is no her except through
me. I am the way, the truth, and the kid.

EXISTENTIAL CRISIS AT 3 AM

There ought to be a word
a word for recognizing
how memory is tidal,
how memory comes back,
back into cycle. If I lay me
down at night, night open
as a black peony, I am preparing
to be salted, and preserved.
At night, I preserve the terrible
dark. I prepare myself to lie down.
If I die, I die in a dead man's float,
dream of _____ .
Just as likely, I fight, I pull
in ways that stab through waves.
Nights like these are called rip tide.
I remember to surrender,
and move shoreward to waking.

You'd call this restlessness—
you'd be mistaken. There are shaky moments
of calm, the sea steadying and gently heaving stars
to shore—a touch of moon, a slant
at cockshut. Speak low, low tide.
I wish I spoke moon. I wish my body
was many fish.
I wish I could find the other side of anything.

You'd call this enough—you'd be mistaken.
Night is worry enough, but dawn is worse.

I am helpless when the men come,
men who have spent years mapping waves
enough to know how best to enter them.

CONVERSATION AMONG DIRT BEFORE RAIN

Let us begin.

Our bargain pews, the chaplain's prayer
(though broken easels of valiant faith)
in the chapel's ark:
the hapless prayer, the anxious prayer,
      irregularities of love and praise
that draw the unfailingly faithful forth.

           Praise sun, praise roof, praise angles of light
           in solemn passing, that penetrate our church.

We smudge the foreheads of rogue tenants
both helplessly bereft and dangerously faithful,
      the judgment house, the callow fold,
a ministry calling all further missionaries
to stagnant dark, where all mishaps turn
appalling and sinful—
is the singular crux, an impotent bluff, a starving
hut that draws its wayward from a hand-pollenated
           wasteland, and forces open serpentine people,
           coruscating as diamonds, sharp and bloody.

Before the Father opens
      the stilted light at every dawn,
we wish for the coronation of water, the farthest
servants, anointed for him:
           the weeds, the barbs,
           the crass, the rakes, the raff—
           we wish to be

the christened brethren and faithful soldiers,
dependent on aerial miracles.

All hovels must have their saints
and their Christly visions. And hell,

languishing hell, makes rapturously ugly
its own plagued virtues.

Sinners are a little hardier than they were.
But we extol infinite supplications and psalms:

virtuous are those
who beneficently chart
the uncharted, the moment the masses were most damned,
fragile, faithless with nonsense,
and so alone,
they accepted and welcome their own redemption.

We had visions in this barren field,
we wished it changed,
worshipped that change, took incremental offerings
of rain in mornings tempestuous and sallow,
the shift from farm to forgotten. We had a Lord

who propelled us to seek water.
We were that Lord,
we were that soil, that farm, the forgotten.

AFTER TIME HAS RUMPLED THE SHEETS OF YOUR MOUTH

When I am winter, shutting privately down in my own deep snow,
allow me solace in stinking rooms of books, typewriters cold and dressed
for procession. Great old ghosts grousing on stairwells, tumblers in cuff

and not a kind word on their paper lips. Allow me mercy in my frozen
thicket, where parties will have come to call and left to hibernate, leaving behind
small tracks of silent pears, tepid angels in wakeful repose.

& allow me comforts—sliced quince, an avocado churned by spoon,
port in crystal tasting of exquisite girls, black cherries, a photograph smoldering
magenta. Leave me hopeful for another. Waiter! *Another.*

III.

Hometowns

"And the window let the light in
until the sun failed in the branches
and, like mercy,
darkness smothered the town."

—KEVIN PRUFER

YOU CAN LEAD A HORSE TO WATER. REPEAT.

I want to say, you're good girls,
wanting to leave your names behind like that.
—Louise Glück

I'll tell you
     I'm a working girl, I'm a *girlfriend experience*.
     I dance incurably and damned on stage.

I'll tell
     you I love you more than the moon.
     You hang it, I'll shoot it.

I'll say I
     adore you more than it orbits,
     blanks out, steals the diamond
     dartle from the sun.

I'll say, point
     me to that old swoln rock,
     and fly me there. I'm over it.

The truth is,
     I mist my panties with a spray bottle.

The truth is,
     I rarely see the sky at night.

I've been ridden hard, and put away aching.
     That thing about horses is false.
     You can give them salt, and they will take it
     willingly. They can't forsake salt.
     They lick it until they blister, and then
     they wear it proud, but secret, inside
     their mouths.

HOME

He hits and hits. It's hitting season,
and we've all come to watch. It's high-risk.
He could get caught trying to steal.
He could be off-base, shooting
for another man's place like that.
He looks discouraged. We sing
take me out. Everyone is singing.
Everyone is eating fistfuls
of peanuts and crackerjacks. He hits.
He gets a fly, by luck. We call this 'out'.
He signals to a second man—they will cheat
a third. He hits and hits. He hits a man,
and the man must walk. He strikes,
but does not, himself, get to walk.
He fouls. He fouls over and over. We feel
bad about his fouling. We sing
Root root root for the home. Home has plates
for everyone, and one diamond.
Home has many men. Home is divided.
Getting there is dirty, and requires hitting
but not striking. It requires switching sides,
and throwing curves. It requires cheating.
The point is: a man gets to go home.
This is called winning.

NIGHT ON MEMORY'S CONVOY, OR, OHIO

Silent, I feel the shadowy mass of Ohio
lean a broad chest upon the window;
silent, the train serpents through onyx
heartland—long blurs of black.
      This is the sea the Midwest knows.

I know nothing of Ohio, only
that it's a place I have not searched,
that remains unturned. Here and everywhere,
your face fogs the glass: a sudden, shifting bog.
      In memory, you and I have wintered

every December's petulant tantrum,
and we have missed the breaking blossoms
of milestone and notches. I wait
for you every season to arrive.
      You must be exactly like Ohio,

at song in every damning corner
of its impressive girth. I will say it
again: Mother, there is war
in this life, everywhere trenches lie open
      to those who fight for you,

who walk by them in the night's dark edifices
unprepared and disillusioned. Tell me
as I see you in everything black enough
to be reflective: that you will come back,
      that this heartland will someday thaw.

We had been taught to sit still, when asked
for the salt, the pepper, the brandy, the knife.
To cut small, and eat smaller. To be seeable, so
that eyes follow in the street, and heads roll
for tiny crimes. To speak softly, and commit
trespasses of faintness. To be nothing
but a thumbprint on a pages of words, written
by giants. There are none of us here. We've died.
And when we haven't, we've suffered
worse: a small blip on memory's seismograph,
an unfathomable, frantic set of lines, gone red red red.

MY GRANDMOTHER TELLS ME OF DEPRESSION-ERA OREGON

The night the town was cremated, boys and girls
laughed there, and gathered what they could
to wear. They made such prancing. No Depression,
just a dance, and an abundance of blackberry wine.
                              Boys were boys where girls were girls.
Food was food. Merriment was just so. We
made ourselves a carousel of curtsies, oh!
It was fun! It had been a bright night, a perfect night,
to sit in a crowded room
                    and allow a flock of dresses
                                        to swallow us whole.
Sis was in another town, with a boy
                    a real man's man, she said. He wanted
to drive a Greyhound bus, she said.
When we were born, we were two inside a great egg,
and we ate what we had. It was enough.
We'd made no vows, except to leave our farm,
our ravaged town. I wish I'd thought to start
the first flame, to catch the world with flint
                    to sow a wish of burning fields.
It was only livelihood, our lonely dark.
The sun must have caught the hem of wheat
on its way out of work, and as the fire grew
we abandoned our dance, our fields, our drunkenness
                         to lie in the river, with sleeping sheep.
When we were born, my mother said,
                    it was a heat wave
and our town was plagued with rolling sweat.
Even the animals fretted in their stalls.
                    To cool herself, she kept us far from her—

Dead mom is many things, but always dead. Nothing
kills a conversation like a dead mom. What are you,

                                        dead mom? Whatever
is left of you is what I pray to. Dead mom makes lunches.
Dead mom is the man on the corner with two cigarettes. Dead
mom wanders the hallways at night, eating pickles from a jar.
I call out for you by your rightful name, dead mom, every time
you die. Dead mom, you die every day. You move, and bury yourself
next to me. Dead mom, you would sleep if you could, but dead moms don't
sleep, they burn. Dead mom, I eat ashes to know what heaven does
to the body. Nobody reads poetry, especially not dead moms,
but dead moms hand out tickets at theaters, they bag groceries, they turn
their heads just so, so in the right light they reflect off of everything.
The marquee is always showing dead mom. Let me live, dead mom.
Forget roses. Forget forget-me-nots. Forget bulbs that wait forever
to finally shoot into recognition months later. Plant rows and rows
of dead mom, because it will seed like crazy, and you will never be able to kill it.

ETIQUETTE

I once put my fist inside someone,
fist the size of a heart,
into someone who was looking
for a heart for herself.

I am not a particularly nice girl—

I plant carrots, and pull them
too early. They make sweet
suckling sounds, like whimpers,
a sucking of breath.

I've been careless. I've left
diaries on trains, stockings
in bathrooms, my smell
on something casual. I've been
casual. I've caused casualties.

My granddaddy is a man of God.
He drove a busted truck, the color
of menses, through Death Valley.
Hundreds of miles, to give
the word of quenching light
to the parched. That must be nice.

MEDITATION ON A LOST PHOTO BOOTH PICTURE

I am waiting for the sun to rise, without any knowledge/ or indication
where my window faces/ in regards to it. I don't know this place, have
never/ been here before. It is very much/ like planning a trip to a place
you refuse to see pictures of/ beforehand, or meeting people/ whose faces
you see only after writing to for a very long time./ Everywhere I go, I
bring two pictures of my parents,/ both in their late twenties, as I am now.
In one,/ they are in a photo booth I think I recognize/ as one from a mall
outside of Palo Verde, though it is impossible/ to say. My dad is wearing
a ball cap and eating a fistful/ of blue cotton candy, and my mother is
laughing joyfully/ in front of him. She looks to be sitting on his lap./ She
is thin here, and sick, but grinning/ my grandfather's grin. Her blouse
is lacey and cream-colored./ Her glasses are in the style of Sally Jessy
Rafael,/ as was popular in 1989. The picture is small, /maybe one by two
inches, one in a series/ that has mostly been lost now. The framing of it—/
my dad in the background and my mother laughing/ at the camera—is
spectacular. How many seconds/ were there between flashes? Did they
plan the faces/ they'd make? Did they pass/ by the booth and decide to
go in, or was the purpose/ of their visit? Though I am not there, I feel
the center/ of there, of theirs. As if they knew, preemptively, that they
would not be able/ to see me in this unfamiliar place, at the desk of my
life,/ and thought to take this picture so that they, too, might participate.
I know this/ is self-indulgent. I know this is arrogant. I know/ these are
stories I tell myself as I fall asleep, fearing death or impermanence./ They
were maybe on a date, while I slept at a sitter's./ But now that I think of
it, was I there? The more I look/ at the picture, the more I remember: I
had ordered/ a milkshake at Johnny Rocket's. The waitress's roller skates/
were blue. We had ridden the carousel, and somewhere/ in my deceptive
frontal cortex, there is/ a one by two inch photograph of all three of us,
and then a memory is born.

ONE IN A LINE OF MANY

for Eloise Klein Healy

What is it, anyway, that fills you
if not matter in a void? I never wanted
to be one of those lesbian poets
who writes about their mothers—*So don't*
she says, and the line goes dead.
What is the mole hill without the mole,
a kitchen table without placemats, Sunday
without the phone? This is a time when most
are making long-distance calls if they have to
and driving over for dinner if they don't.
Add an 's', and it smothers, is what I'm telling myself.
That reliable absence is a way to know
you come from everything. This way,
you make the map and the legend.

Today people, grown and not, are walking in stride
with bodies who bore them, who bear them still,
who bear them empty, who say they are the promise
of everything, the gift of wanting, who let the phone ring
once before answering, *I'm here.*

TO THE LARKS, WHO KNOW NOTHING OF WHAT WE DO

for Charlotte Mew

In truth, we came after, and thus it was easier.

In truth, my thumbs press the grass.

In truth, you are buried under grass, and it has grown over you.

In truth, there is no grave at all.

In truth, this is a poem, and what I am touching

is a frogging artery in your poem's bicep.

In truth, you search for larks from the grave of your poem.

In truth, you never got to love a woman, and I have loved many.

In truth, I have been greedy with my love, my love is a big

fuck you. In truth, your body went madly home, from love's torched face.

In truth, one day the quiet earth may give it back.

In truth, this is the end of all roads, and you ripple,

soft and discontent from praising the birding calls.

In truth, the birds are women. In truth, the grass is women.

In truth, the bicep, the body, the grave, are women.

I write your stanza's decomposing bones.

MORE OR LESS

The inhabitants of the bus more or less cared
about destination: that it was coming,
that it loomed, and even, in some cases,
that it arrive as quickly as possible.

On certain nights, more or less,
the driver could see dusk smearing
up the horizon like exaggerated, tragic mascara.
He wondered who in the world would have painted
such a scene, the landscape faceless, eyeless—

Suppose a woman lived there, in the spaces
between light and silhouette. A whole sky,
more or less, of women, small as you could paint them,
alone or lonely or just shadow,
and the marvelous mockery of the road,
winding by and away from them?

Would I be there? I am always
inserting myself. The invitation said *plus one*,
which subtracts the more or less obvious.
Situation multiplied, you'd be carrying one
to the bathroom after a long night of wine.
The equation simple, and divisive.
Something unspoken to the power
of something stated. What a rotten formula.

Since I am already here uninvited,
I'll be the Queen of more than
lesser country, dress caught in the wheel.
I cannot move. Bury me in this dress,
in the first-song fields, in summer,
when the wheat falls in love with wind.

HOW DO I LOVE THEE? LET ME COUNT THE WAYS.

for Nicolo Grelli

Once, we walked all the way across the Brooklyn Bridge
in a rainstorm.
               You, too, had been battling
a world, from another side of it. We were company enough.
Three times the bridge stuttered
                    as if to slump. For you
I knitted it stable with superstition:
                     I walk in a straight line,
I know all the words to *My Country 'Tis of Thee*, I conjure a copy of myself
as a toddler, tenaciously pursuing a pudding cup.
We walked five miles without regarding miles
                    to Sixth Avenue, where you swallowed
seven cookies repetitiously. One, then one other. It did not rebound us to
                        zero, it broke you
from your body as easily as bread. You could see
we were both soaked and suffering, considerably less so
                       together. You ate. I traced
a wall, where someone inscribed "Tina takes it in the butt at 9 AM."
What worries me about Manhattan is this: everyone
strolls selfishly with ten cigarettes in their pockets, with
                      no sense of sharing.
I share with you Tina's number, should you find yourself someday
awake at that hour. You're more like Rufus Wainwright,
your late-night birthright,
               bumbling from bed at 11:11,
with *Good Morning America*. Those mornings we were
anything but regular people, humbled
               by our own spectrum of possible deaths.
Would it be cheating, would it cheapen, if we joined
our twelve friends who'd given up ghosts?

                    Were thirteen and fourteen so unlucky?
We don't die—this is a poem—but I've misplaced numbers
somewhere. My brother, I am not accountable. I cheat. Now I inhabit
a place where the snow slogs on before I wake,
                            erasing all our work

IN THIS STORY, I AM ORPHEUS

The cotton appears as a vision:
thorn apple. Moon flower. I hide
from in a field for years. I lay myself
down at eleven, though the planes know
I am there. They tell me the women are close.

I am dirt, now. I eat potato bugs. I fall
in love with a puddle where a girl lives.
I am fifteen. I make a pact to save her.
I search for a God to pinky promise.
I search for someone who might grant me entry.

I am nineteen. I have not reached
the underworld. I have lived all my life
as a crop, and have believed myself free.
My girl has dried up, gained entry to the sky instead.
I hide here, because I know the world. I do not wish to join it.

I search again for God, and he brings
only a shower of sulfur. I am touched
by God and his pesticide mercy. I am twenty
when the world breaks in. I am sleeping
when they attack, these Maenads, women of rivers.

They slay me. They take my crop.
They do not show the grace of God, but tear
my limbs like cotton. Bury me, oh beasts,
in these fields, that I may be forever unknown.
Instead, I rest at Eagle Mountain, where birds have never been louder.

EPILOGUE

Are you ready, asphalt? For the buck,
the rodeo of cracks, the last activity
you may bear witness to? When did you
last see rain, and where did it go,
                          bladder clouds full?
The heat will always be irrational, always
with slight relief at darkness, when the heavens open
a spectacular velvet dress and show us
their stars, or show nothing
their stars. Eagle Mountain is a ghost town, now.
Daylight on Route 60, apricot and lovely,
goes undiscussed, but for the crickets
and the terrible songs they sing.
                     They sing: come home,
                     they sing, never be ashamed.
All night they sing, and if we could, we'd feel
that good, hymnal feeling of nothing new—

NOTES ON TEXT

"Love Arrived May Find Us Someplace Else" is a closing line from Elizabeth Jennings' poem "Delay."

"To the larks, who know nothing of what we do" is a wild variation on a line by Charlotte Mew, from her poem "Fame."

"Donner Pass, 2012" utilizes a line from C.D. Wright's poem, "Nothing to Declare": "hearts go bad/ like something open on a shelf."

"Dead Mom, or How News Travels in a Small Town" is written with thanks to Szymborska's poem "Identification."

ACKNOWLEDGEMENTS & PREVIOUS PUBLICATIONS

This manuscript would not have been possible without the generosity of friends, community, and literary fellowships. It feels impossible to name everyone, but here is a good start: my editor Ann Dernier, for her inspired and eagle-eyed dedication to the manuscript. Kevin Prufer, Eloise Klein Healy, and Sharon Bryan for their eternal mentorship, good humor, and wild love of poetry. Lizz Ehrenpreis for almost twenty years of Leo loyalty. The Lesley crew of Eve Linn, Boston Gordon, Aimee Noel, and Shari Caplan for their encouragement and levity. Pamela Petro for her oracle wisdom and heart of gold. My partner, AC Panella, for having the most beautiful brain, and keeping me supplied with ginger snaps.

Thank you to the Tennessee Williams Foundation, the Vermont Studio Center, the Lambda Literary Foundation, Dickinson House, and the Tom and Evelyn Newberry Fellowship, for the endowments that made it possible to work tirelessly on this manuscript.

Eternal thanks and eternal rest to Mr. Nick McClellan, the first person to introduce me to poetry.

"After Time Has Rumpled the Sheets of Your Mouth" *Barely South Review*.

 "Home" (under "Domestic Violence"), "Obituary of an Unknown Woman" (under the name "[it turns out it's someone you almost knew]"), and "Dead Mom" (under the name "Canopy"), "Donnor Pass, 2012" (originally "[and then the rain chatted down on the train at Donner Pass]"), and "To the larks, who know nothing of what we do" *Adrienne*.

"Ars Poetica" (under the name "The Last Five Years") was originally published in *The Tahoma Review*.

"Death and the School Bus" and "Heaven, That Day Old Bread" *Eleven Eleven*.

"Poem in Which I Rewrite History" (under the name "First Girlfriends") *Fourth River*.

"Saguaros", "Chopin's Funeral March", and "There is No Room for Jesus in This City" (originally "Just imagine the city is like a trench") *Elective Affinities*.

"Home" *The National Poetry Review*.

"Dead Mom Reprise" "You Can Lead a Horse to Water. Repeat." and "Cootie Catcher" *Thin Noon*.

"Crop Dusters" *The Cimarron Review*.

"Wake" "Trailer Trash" and "Epilogue" *Tupelo Quarterly*.

July Westhale is a poet and essayist living in Oakland, CA. She is the author of *Trailer Trash* (winner of the 2016 Kore Press Book Award), *The Cavalcade* (Finishing Line Press), and *Occasionally Accurate Science* (Nomadic Press). Her poems are published in numerous journals, magazines, and anthologies.

A small town California native, her work deals primarily with broken landscapes, and the intersections between personal narrative and collective consciousness. She writes extensively about class and trauma, in both her poetry and her prose.

Her nonfiction has appeared in the *Huffington Post, Autostraddle*, and *The Establishment*, and has been nominated for *Best American Essays*. She is indebted to the Vermont Studio Center, the Tom and Evelyn Newbury Grant, the Raveel Grant, Dickinson House, Sewanee, and the Lambda Literary Foundation for their generous support of her work.

She is currently at work on a second children's book about coping with difficult political landscapes, and a graphic novel about queer femme friendships.

When she's not writing, she teaches Creative Writing, History, and English at Cogswell College. In addition, she works in reproductive health as an educator and patient advocate.

She has an MFA in Poetry from Lesley University.

ABOUT THE PRESS

 As a community of literary activists devoted to bringing forth a diversity of voices through works that meet the highest artistic standards, Kore Press publishes women's writing that deepens awareness and advances progressive social change.

Kore has been publishing the creative genius of women since 1993 in Tucson, to ensure more equitable public discourse and take action toward establishing a more inclusive, democratic, and accurate historic record.

- Since its inception in 1923, *Time Magazine* has had one female editor.

- Since 1948, the Pulitzer Prize for Poetry has gone to 51 men and 19 women.

- Only twelve of 109 Nobel Prizes for Literature have gone to women. Three of the twelve female winners were in the last decade.

Become a literary activist and support feminist, independent publishing by purchasing books directly from the publisher, by making a tax-deductible contribution to Kore, or becoming a member of the Press. Please visit us at korepress.org.

ABOUT THE KORE PRESS FIRST BOOK AWARD IN POETRY

This competition is open each year to any female writer who has not published a full-length collection of poetry. Writers who have had chapbooks of less than 42 pages printed in editions of no more than 400 copies are eligible.

Past winners and judges:

2015 *Body Burden* by Zayne Turner
Judge-Tracie Morris

2014 *Silent Anatomies* by Monica Ong
Judge-Joy Harjo

2013 *River Legs* by Jen McClanaghan
Judge-Nikkey Finny

2011 *Double Agent* by Michelle Chan Brown
Judge-Bhanu Kapil

2010 *Love and the Eye* by Laura Newbern
Judge-Claudia Rankine

2009 *Something in the Potato Room* by Heather Cousins
Judge-Patricia Smith

2008 *Souvenirs of a Shrunken World* by Holly Iglesias
Judge-Harryette Mullen

2007 *Benjamin's Spectacles* by Spring Ulmer
Judge-Sonia Sanchez

2006 *Loveliest Grotesque* by Sandra Lim
Judge-Marilyn Chin

2005 *Errant Thread* by Elline Lipkin
Judge-Eavan Boland

2004 *Various Modes of Departure* by Deborah Fries
Judge-Carolyn Forché

2003 *Rigging the Wind* by Jennifer Barber
Judge-Jane Miller

To purchase titles, go to www.KorePress.org